Win at Office Politics

A Beginner's 30-Minute Quick Start Guide

Table of Contents

Introduction

I want to thank you and congratulate you for investing in this quick start guide.

If you are working in any organization with more than just a handful of people, you will be bound to encounter politics. The working world is a dangerous place, filled with backstabbing individuals who could care less about anyone or anything other than their own success up the corporate ladder.

To navigate this tricky and dirty world of office politics, you must develop a strong game plan and be aware of risks. Office Politics: How to Survive and Thrive in the Dirty Game of Office Politics outlines concisely the various ways you can not only navigate but truly thrive in this type of work environment.

Thanks again for downloading this guide, I hope you enjoy it!

Chapter 1 – Why Play the Game?

A workplace thriving with backstabbers, gossipers, bullying cliques, suck-ups (basically the people you hate in the office!) can put unwarranted stress to people who just want to go about their career clean. This may or may not be news for you, but the game of office politics is a game played in EVERY office. The difference lies in whether the game is played for the benefit of the company or for the benefit of the chosen few.

Naturally, different people react differently when confronted by this reality. Some are born to the dance of politics and thrive. Others try to play the game only to be swallowed by the bigger, more ruthless fish. Some shy away from all the stress of politics and focus on high performance only to see later on that their less competent but influential colleague stole the promotion that is rightfully theirs. There are others who are just plain disgusted with the game and actively avoid getting caught in the murky world of office politics.

For most people who do not like or fail to thrive in the presence of office politics, pursuing their careers in a different office environment is always a looming option only to be confronted by the sad reality that dirty politics still haunt the "greener side" of the lawn. While everyone acknowledges the presence of office politics in every cubicle of every office, there is much disagreement on whether to advocate active participation or to avoid it completely. However, most find the safest place to be in the middle ground – knowing how to play the game and navigate so you can protect yourself while not really actively participating.

While adopting this anonymous-but-ready stance is tempting, it is easy to get caught up when confrontation arises. This means that if you really want to survive and thrive, you need to participate and pick a side. The political landscape in every office is unique and you cannot trust anybody so whose side should you play with? Yourself of course! Politics flourish when individuals with different interests engage in power struggles.

If you do not define your interests, you will eventually and inevitably be reduced to a mere pawn for the most cunning of players or even worse, a stepping stone. When you finally realized that your talents have been used and abused by other people for their own ends, you will feel cheated and disillusioned which may lead to less enthusiasm in doing your job which can impair your performance and destroy future opportunities to further your career.

This DOES NOT, in any way, mean that you have the license to be self-serving. When a player only has the desire to further his/her own ends, he/she will gain many faceless enemies that would want to expose the player's self-serving nature. Self-serving players are also a bane in the company's growth as they would commonly use the company's valuable resources for their benefits alone and spread hate and dissent among the company's ranks.

So how do you avoid this fall to the dark side? Align your interests with your company's vision, mission and interests. This way, no one will question your integrity and intentions. Remember, as your company grows, your chance for career growth also increases. If you improve your craft, your company will certainly profit from it as well. Also, the prevalence of dirty politics in the office does not mean that traits like honesty, sincerity and integrity are not valued.

On the contrary, the presence of these values is an important ingredient in the recipe for success of truly successful people. Besides, contrary to what is always portrayed in fiction, pretending to be someone who has good intentions is more difficult to pull off in the long run. People are NOT ALWAYS stupid and eventually, they will see through the ruse. So in essence, instead of hiding behind a lie that you want to bring your company (and your team) to success with you, live the lie until it becomes your truth!

The presence of office politics, especially if competent company assets (whose career is built upon the company's core values and best interest) are involved can be beneficial for the company. This means that if an influential player deems the participation in a key project important to further his/her own career, he/she can bring other employees (not only those who are under his/her sphere of influence but rivals as well) to participate in the project, increasing the chance that the key project will be executed with high quality. In the end, if the project is executed well, this can grant promotion to the employee/s involved, bring more money to the company and make customers satisfied. Everybody happy!

This "everybody happy" approach is what the book is trying to make the reader understand and emulate in advocating participation in office politics. Humans are social animals. Admit it or not, we have our weaknesses and we mask these weaknesses by working with other people who happen to be good at what we hate to do.

Good and lasting working relationships are formed when you resist the urge to always "take" from a professional relationship, that is, when you adopt a compromise where you, your partner (or teammates) and the company will all benefit.

A common mistake of "cunning players" is to always maximize the benefits from a venture by hoarding all the glory and credit for themselves. In the end, these players end up to be the most hated person in the office, his/her more cunning enemies patiently waiting (or worse, planning) for his/her downfall.

Office politics is a reality that each employee (from the bottom dwellers to the top dogs) must face every day. The greatest pain that dirty politics brings to people are the feelings of being manipulated and coerced to do something for the benefit of other people – making the other side win at the expense of your loss. Truly successful players seek to make everybody with competing interests win without being a pleaser, that is, if you want to survive and thrive, learn to always find common ground where everybody will be satisfied.

Chapter 2 – The Rule of 10

The political landscape is unique for every office so you cannot expect that what might have worked in one office will work in your office. Still, there are basic rules that you must abide by if you want to play and succeed in the game of office politics. It is not always: ***When you play the game of thrones, you win or you die. There is no middle ground*** scenario as the Game of Thrones character, Cersei Lannister bluntly puts it. Besides the fact that no one has to die in your office (although it is perfectly understandable if you really want someone to die), remember that "winning" involves finding a common ground for all and your ultimate goal is to be a respected and productive asset for your company - not a cut-throat who stabs people at the back when the lights are out.

Abiding by these rules will keep you from resulting to low and dirty tactics that characterize destructive office politics. Be reminded that not all people in your office know these rules so you cannot expect them to fight like how you do. This does not mean, however, that you cannot anticipate their every move and protect yourself from their attacks.
Here are the basic rules of the game of office politics every player should abide to:

1. Survey the playing field: Spheres of Influence

Before entering the political arena, you should be able to form a rough mental picture of the whole political scenario in your office. The dynamics of power play in the office must be clear to you. Always ask: Who has the power over whom?

Whether you know this already or not, it is worth to explicitly state that power in an office is measured by how much influence you have more than anything else. Looks, talent, money and your status can help you garner influence but these can never be equated with influence per se.

There are offices when the most influential person is not the boss. In this case, true power resides on that person as he/she can influence his/her very boss' decisions.

You can say that you have influence over a person if that person considers your whims and even your presence when they make a decision. Commonly, these decisions will be in your favor as they don't want to rouse you or go against you (well at least head-on.) The bigger your sphere of influence, the more you have a say in the events in the office, the more powerful you are!

Each person in the office will have spheres of influence that you have to assess. Some will have big spheres of influence encompassing even the bosses; some will have limited influence while some will have none. It is important to understand how each major player affects the power balance in the office.

For example, in your office, a certain Martha has a wide sphere of influence excluding a certain clique. If Martha can influence the leader of that clique, then there is a chance that all the members of that clique will inevitably be included in her sphere, whether they like it or not (assuming that the leader of the clique has influence to his/her members).

Knowing the extent of influence of major players have in the office and how they use their influence can help you calculate events in the office and use them to your advantage. Using Martha again as an example, if your department needs the participation of all employees in a project where you are the project leader, it would do well if you have a nice, professional, non-hostile relationship with Martha. If you can get her to participate, chances are, her whole sphere will follow her.

Now, if Martha suddenly gets relocated to another department, the void that her sphere of influence will leave behind is called a power vacuum. Two scenarios can happen here: either someone will fill the void and be the new Martha or others will have a chance to expand their spheres of influence dividing the department. If you are keen enough, you can help an influential friend install himself/herself in the void left by Martha. If successful, you will have an indirect influence to the events in your office via your friend. Or better yet, you can work to fill the void yourself or expand your own sphere.

As was said in Chapter 1, people are not always stupid. However, let us admit it. Most of the time, people have the tendency to make unwise decisions. Your boss is not immune to this fact. While the presence of cliques and people who are more influential than the boss can be normal, its unchecked presence is a sign of poor central leadership. The void left by weak leadership allows cliques, groups and people who exert too much influence to thrive.

If you are a manager or executive or someone who vies for those positions, be aware of this sign of weakness. Regardless of who is the most influential person in the office, it should be your priority not to get into your boss' bad side and show your competence.

2. Know when to strike

Cunning is a trait always associated with dedicated players of the game. Being cunning means that you can see opportunities to thrive when what all other people see are setbacks. However, it is not enough that you are able to identify opportunities that you can take advantage of. You should be able transform these opportunities into results by always taking action when it is necessary. According to Sun Tzu's military book The Art of War, if you do not see a possible opportunity in a situation, then you are stupid. If you see an opportunity but fail to act on it because of doubt, then you are a coward.

An example in the first rule involving Martha involves taking advantage of what happened to her. It should be noted that Martha relocating happened not as a result of any intervention from a player. In these situations, never hesitate to strike. If Martha's relocation is the direct result of meddling from a player, it would be better to proceed with caution to avoid being identified as a co-conspirator. Knowing when to take action and when to take caution is a skill learned through experience but being insightful and thinking out of the box is a good starting point.

Never attempt to create opportunities by tarnishing a colleague's reputation. This will raise red flags particularly if done blatantly. Always try to settle a competition in a win-win situation as was emphasized in chapter 1.

3. Forge alliances!
Allies, taken into the context of office politics are individuals who share with you the same interests that can make them more likely aid you in times of need. Forging alliances can widen your sphere of influence dramatically. You may be revolting at the thought of "befriending" people you do not like, but remember also that inside the office, relationships must be kept professional. How else could people bear to stand the stinky and dirty politics in an office? It is not like they love it. It is because they want to keep their jobs to feed their family.

You do not have to like people to be able to maintain a healthy working relationship with them. People make the mistake of investing too much emotion on interpersonal relationships made inside the office, only to find out that their "friends" have just "used" them. Emotional attachment may build camaraderie, but too much can set unnecessary expectations which can end up on permanently sundered working relationships.

Never hesitate to give your smile and extend your helping hand to all but take special care to know and make acquaintances on influential people and people whom you share common interests with.

However, do not overdo this. If people sensed that you are just selectively good to those you like or those who are "up there", your officemates can easily brand you as a user and you will have a hard time earning their trust. That is why you need to be good to ALL.

As pointed out earlier, no matter how talented you are, there are still some tasks where you will need the help of other people who are more capable of doing it. This is where your network of pleasant and professional relationships comes to play.

Another reason why you should be good to all is the fact that alliances need to be re-forged especially if power vacuums form and power struggles arise. When people whom you share common interests with suddenly change priorities or becomes promoted or re-located, a big network of people will serve your interests well.

You may also be tempted to think that if the concept of allies exists in the game of office politics, then there must also be enemies. You are dead wrong about that. Branding people who do not share your beliefs is a sign of immaturity. While people whom you share common interests with are handy to be around, you should not shun from building relationships with those who do not believe in your beliefs. Doing so prevents your growth and the opportunity to learn from them.

Knowing these people and their beliefs will also allow you to offer compromises that will bring both of you in a win-win situation in case working with them is inevitable (emphasis again on being good to ALL.) Make sure that you set boundaries when you treat people nicely. Never lose the power to say no. Being nice to everybody does not mean that you have to attend to every call for help. This is obviously not possible. If you do try to attend to each request, then expect to be "burnt out".

4. Trust no one but yourself

In the game of office politics, never assume that everyone who is smiling at you likes you. There is no way to know who's who until they show their cards. In fact, there is a common saying that an enemy would hide his dagger behind his smile. While we do not want to brand anybody as an enemy, the same cannot be said for other people. They may brand you as a threat because you do not share their interests. These people will patiently wait for you to commit a mistake, if not work actively in the shadows to sabotage you.

For this reason, being strictly professional in the workplace also extends to keeping your personal life private. These people will seek to undermine your efforts and concentration by blowing even the slightest flaw in your personal life to epic proportions. Even just a small hint that your marriage is on the rocks can spread gossips that are twisted by malice.
Never divulge any personal information that can be used against you. Maintaining strictly professional relationships with people you do not trust and trusting only those who have proven their loyalty can accomplish this. You should also manage your social media accounts. These are potential sources of information regarding your personal life and people will inevitably stalk your profile.

Avoid venting your problems in your social media accounts or better yet, make separate accounts for office use. That way, you can control the flow of information about your life without having to avoid "adding friends" in your accounts.

If your coworkers do happen to add you on Facebook, be sure to put them on the "work" list and limit what they can see on your timeline. You do not want them to know too much about your personal life.

5. Avoid hostilities
Confrontations involving yelling and emotions must be avoided especially in public. Knowing that you are right does not give you the license to confront and be hostile to the other party. Commonly, when your boss mediates and asks what happened, most of your allies will refuse to take sides especially if the matter being discussed is shrouded by controversy. Do not take this personally, if you are in their situation, what will you do? If the other party is the one who is aggressive, being calm and refusing to be provoked will tell people that you are emotionally secure and mature, making them more likely think that you are right.

6. Always uphold your part of the bargain

Favors and returning favors are the currency used in the game of office politics. Always uphold your end of the bargain and it will portray you as someone who is honorable and sincere. This can do great things in your sphere of influence. This also communicates the message to your colleagues that you are willing to make compromises when needed because they will not see you as someone who enjoys taking while avoiding giving. This will make it easier for you to negotiate with people who do not share your interests and ideals.

7. Be subtle

Take care not to get carried away with playing the game and overdo it. This can lead people to branding you as a "full-time politician" or worse, as a lowly meddler, gossiper, backstabber etc. You will have a hard time exerting your influence if you get branded negatively because people will think that they are being manipulated. You know that you are playing the game well when people forget that you are actually playing. This is where the art of subtlety must be perfected. Never be too blatant when taking advantage of situations and building good professional relationships especially with your superiors.

8. Back-up your skill in playing the game with competence

Some people who actively use "low-blows" when playing the game of office politics are actually insecure of their lack of talent that is why they do everything to sabotage excellent performers. To avoid being flagged as such, improve your craft and show everyone that you are competent whenever the appropriate situation presents itself. Competence is also your fail safe when your schemes do not work and the odds are against you.

For example, try not to ask too many questions. The more you ask, the more you reveal that you are not aware of what is going in the office. You want to create an aura of mystery at all times, an external appearance as if you are aware of what is going on everywhere within the office.

9. Leave office politics in the office!

The last thing that you want is for the negativity of the office place to haunt you at home. If you are going crazy in the office, then your home is your last safe haven so do not let the choking miasma of politics follow you at home. Obsession on scheming and plotting can take away quality time spent with your family. For some of you, improving the financial situation of your family is the main driving factor in engaging in the game of office politics. Everything will be for naught if you lose your family along the way. Remember that in the office, you may never know who are true to their word but your family is sure to never leave you no matter what.

10. Never lose yourself!

Always remember your values and goals and do not forget who you are. It is easy to change when you get caught up in the web of lies and deceit of other people. Sticking to your goals and values lets you focus on the more important things, preventing your emotions to get the best of you.

Chapter 3 – Steel Yourself

People who say that the world is a dangerous place have never been inside an office. When people get cornered or fail to get what they want, they start to play the game of office politics dirty, acting like sociopaths disregarding morals and ethics. When the game is reduced to this rubbish, and you are determined to stay and weather everything, you need to protect yourself with an iron will. Here are some tips to become a strong-willed player of the game:

Be more confident by honing your skills. Most people who shy away from playing the stressful game of office politics are those who have confidence issues and low self-esteem. You should work hard to increase your sense of self-worth by honing your talents and skills. Some people have a tendency to bully others when they sense that you are someone that they can just push around and manipulate. Conducting yourself in a confident manner and backing that confidence with competence can deter most bullying attempts.

Use your weaknesses to your advantage. As Tyrion Lannister, the most popular Game of Thrones character, puts it: ***Never forget what you are. The rest of the world will not. Wear it like an armor and it can never be used to hurt you.*** Sometimes, your difficulties and circumstances can give you an edge when playing the game. Doing this prevents your enemies from using it against you. Instead of lamenting that you graduated from an anonymous college while your competitors got a master's degree in Harvard, advertise it and show them that even if you studied from a mediocre business school, your experience, attitude and willingness to learn more than makes up for that fact.

Be a team player and widen your network. Everyone always has their own agenda somewhere in their sleeve. They may not show it but when opportunities arise, they will grab it to further their own interests.

Knowing this fact, some people make a mistake of assuming that everyone is so selfish that working with them is not possible. These people will typically keep to themselves and work in isolation, thinking that they can work their way to the top alone. You will need the help of other people somewhere along the way and isolating yourself will be counter-productive. Isolate yourself and you will fall easy prey to manipulators and bullies.

The strongest professional relationships (and sometimes friendships) are forged when people work with each other under pressure.

Why? Because chances are, people will reveal their true nature and drop all pretenses when subjected to pressure. When you are a team player, you do not just help yourself and other people further your interests, you are also identifying genuine people from the pretenders.

Chapter 4 – Dealing with Threats

It is inevitable that you will encounter people who will do just about everything to get what they want. While it is very tempting to use their own devious devices against them, you should think twice to do this.

Remember rule #10: Never forget who you are! While people who do whatever it takes do get what they want at the end of the day, true success is only bestowed to those who still retain the moral values they started with before playing the game of office politics. You cannot call yourself a success if every single person in the office hates you!

The political jungle is never complete without the ruthless predators. Here are some tips to prevent you from falling prey to these hungry and desperate people while minimizing the risk of becoming one of them:

Manipulators – If you feel that an influential player is trying to manipulate you, think about the circumstances if you resist and the things that you can benefit from if you don't. Instead of running away or becoming hostile, look at possible opportunities that you can take advantage of so both of you will benefit from the manipulation. At some point, influential people in the office will try to manipulate the smaller fish.

Just go with the flow and work towards turning the situation to your advantage. Sometimes, insisting on making a deal with manipulators rather than going with whatever they want you to do will make a manipulator realize that you are no pushover and if he/she wants to take advantage of your talents, then he/she must give something in return.

Brownnosers – Studies suggest that people with authority really have a tendency to fall for brownnosing. Trust your boss to handle this accordingly. If your boss seems to be "falling for it", then identify the reason for brownnosing. Commonly people brownnose because they know they lack competency to compete with top-performers. Always produce results that can outshine the brownnoser's work and let it brownnose for you.

Make it your priority to find whatever it is that you are good at and hone your talents and skills so your boss will have a reason to keep you around by his/her side. From there, character will cement your place on your boss' side. Once you are one of the closest confidants of your boss, you need not worry about brownnosers.

Cliques – Clique members tend to get insecure when a competent beginner rocks the house. They will either force the newbie to submission so that they can make him/her join the clique and they can all feast on the benefits that he/she can provide or bully him/her to oblivion. If you are the newbie, as you are working on your confidence, try to build as many professional relationships as soon as possible to discourage the cliques' advances.

Is being a member of a clique bad for you? Studies suggest yes, they are. Because cliques often exclude people that they don't like, being a member of one can limit your sphere of influence to the other members of your clique only.

If your group does not have a particularly good reputation, then you risk being seen as one of them even if you are not. Be friendly to everyone and if you will surround yourself with people, prefer those who are better than you. This way, you can emulate their good traits and habits.

Gossipers – More obsessed with hoarding information rather than working on improving their careers, the only real deterrent for them is prevention – keep confidential information confidential. What gossipers do not know will not hurt you! Avoid involving yourself in controversies or on scandals that can tarnish your reputation because for gossipers, a small spark is just what it takes to create a forest fire that will destroy your reputation.

Backstabbers – A backstabber's strength is his/her ability to hide in the shadow of being your friend or ally while bleeding you to death. Identifying them may not stop them but this will allow you to evade their efforts in fishing out vital information that they can use against you and flush them out of your professional life. A neat trick to identify a backstabber is to forge a little story about and make several versions of it. Narrate one version each to your suspects and see what rumor will spread. Voila! You have your culprit. Exposing a backstabber will caution people to trusting him/her.

Pseudo-bosses – Pseudo bosses think that they can get to make you work for them as a personal assistant – for free. Unlike the manipulator, pseudo-bosses will try to use more direct methods to take advantage of you. This is where confidence and network can help you. Show that you are no pushover and that you have many friends to back you up.

Thieves – Office politics create thieves of a different kind, one who steals ideas and credits. To not fall prey to this, maintain a close relationship with your boss so you can communicate your ideas directly. Timing is also a factor on this one. Communicate your ideas when your boss or your team is listening and at their full attention, that way, stealing ideas can be prevented.

Make sure to keep logs and documentation of ideas. A nice trick is to update your team via email for any good ideas that may come up from you. That way you can always show them that it was your idea after all. If the thief is a master thief and he/she was able to bypass your safeguards, contact your HR department to report the problem. You can only stop being a victim if you refuse to become one.

Sabotage expert – Sabotage experts undermine the efforts of their competitors either by meddling or by using psychological warfare. A common practice by this person is to tell a top performer that everybody hates the top performer and that their officemates think that the top performer is a brownnoser. This can destroy the momentum of a top performer.

To deter these efforts, you must learn to let go and focus on your work and be confident. If the sabotage expert sees that you are unshaken, he/she will stop. If he/she starts to interfere with your work by constantly providing distractions, go to a place far away from the jerk and try to finish your work. Politely ask for space and some private time or work where the boss can see you.

Conclusion

Thank you again for downloading this guide!
I hope this book was able to help you discover new ways to navigate the tricky world of office politics.

If you enjoyed this guide, please take the time to share your thoughts and post a review on Amazon. It'd be greatly appreciated!

Thank you and good luck!